What the experts are saying about RAMI'S BOOK:

"Rami's Book is like a breath of fresh air, teaching us about our innocence and the simplicity of loving ourselves and others."

—Gerald Jampolsky, M.D. and Diane Cirincione

"We have been taught for a long time that the entrance to God's presence is through the eyes of the child. Rami flings wide that delicious door of perception. Thank you Rami!"

—Rev. Stan Hampson, President, Association of Unity Churches

"Rami's Book is a gift from an angel. The innocent beauty filling these pages brings me tears of joy. I wish children of all ages would read this book."

—Alan Cohen

"Our hope is that all adults as well as children may benefit by the understanding and love that Rami shares in this delightful book."

—Penny and Ken Keyes

"Sensitively and endearingly written ... Rami's innocence and candidness is both moving and refreshing."

—Science of Thought Review, England

*"Of all the books I've reviewed to offer here (hundreds), this one went right to my inner heart and made me cry quite wonderfully. Truly an angelic and marvelous work, and a gift to the child still within me. I put it on display with a sign: 'very,very highly recommended. **** on the goosebump chart!'."*

—Richard Rodgers, manager, The Grateful Heart Bookstore

RAMI'S BOOK

RAMI'S BOOK

The Inner Life of a Child

Written & Illustrated by
Rami Vissell

RAMIRA PUBLISHING

RAMI'S BOOK: The Inner Life of a Child

Copyright 1989 by **RAMIRA PUBLISHING**,
        P.O. Box 1707, Aptos, California 95001.

First printing   January, 1989   5000 copies
Second printing   March, 1991   5000 copies

Library of Congress Catalog Card Number: 88-91345
ISBN: 0-9612720-4-X (Hardcover)

Photo Credits:
Front and back cover photos by Doris Buckley
Pages 16 and 35 by Carla Anette Chotzen
Pages 15, 18, 21, 22 and 28 by Doris Buckley
Page 37 by Barry Vissell

Page 17 story and illustration by Mira Vissell

Typesetting by Polaris Publishing Company
Book and cover design by Josh Gitomer
Printed in singapore by Palace Press

I Dedicate This Book With Love To…

…my family and animals who helped me so much, and
…to all children and grownups everywhere.

I Am Especially Thankful For:

My mom and dad for encouraging me to write this book.
My little sister, Mira, who loves my artwork no matter how good I think it is.
Doris Buckley, who took such beautiful pictures of me and my animal friends.
Josh Gitomer, who did such a great job designing this book.
Bobbi and John Hansen, my dear friends, who typeset this book.
Pumpkin, my cat, who faithfully sat by my side watching me do my illustrations.

Contents

When Rami was four years old, she often sat by our side as we wrote the beginning chapters of our first book, *The Shared Heart*. We enthusiastically shared our joy of writing. We would often tell her, "We just write what is in our hearts."

One day, after silently watching us for some time, Rami decided to "write" her first book: pictures of her baby doll glued together to form a book. Some children play nurse, doctor, teacher or fireman. Rami and Mira have always played author and illustrator. We have volumes of little hand-made books in our home.

Rami illustrated *The Shared Heart* when she was seven years old. At eight and nine years old she wrote several stories as well as a full chapter for our second book, *Models of Love*. Both girls illustrated that book.

Rami began receiving letters of appreciation from children all over the world. They liked her stories in *Models of Love*, and wanted her to write more. One slightly older boy wrote that he used to be angry at everyone, especially his parents, but her stories taught him about love. He was very grateful.

There were many letters from adults too. They said her stories helped them to remember the child within themselves.

So it didn't surprise us when Rami announced on her eleventh birthday that she wanted to write and illustrate her own book. We encouraged her whole-heartedly.

Rami wrote this book throughout her eleventh year of life. Because she was home-schooling at the time, it became her special project. She often discussed her ideas with us, and we helped with sentence structure and grammar, but the ideas, the concepts and the stories are all hers. Before each writing session, she sat silently asking for help from the angels and especially Anjel, her "sister in the heaven world".

Mira, Rami's six year old sister, wanted to be involved too. She "wrote" her own section in the "Families are Wonderful" chapter. Mira was also Rami's most devoted fan-club, patiently waiting to see each new illustration.

Now our whole family is delighted to give the gift of *Rami's Book* to the world. It is our greatest hope that adults as well as children will celebrate the magical inner child which brings us ever closer to the heart of love.

Joyce and Barry Vissell
Aptos, California
Summer, 1988

Loving Yourself

LOVING YOURSELF is important. When you love yourself you feel so good inside and so full of joy. Our best friend can be ourselves. Have you ever hugged yourself? Try it, it feels good! When I was in second grade I traveled a long way to school each day. Sometimes, because my parents couldn't pick me up on time, I stayed in afterschool care. On one of those days the person in charge of afterschool care had to be very busy with some of the first grade children. At first we had a lot of fun, then some of the older kids formed a group and started saying bad things to the younger children. Some of the girls started to cry and others were very unhappy. I felt unhappy too. I realized that it was silly to just stay there. I decided to go off by myself. I found a little trail and followed it a short way to some nice trees. I found a very pretty tree and sat under it. I decided to make grass dolls. I started making up a little story using the dolls. Soon I forgot about all of the bad things the

children were saying and started having lots of fun. When the bell rang for snack, I jumped in surprise and remembered where I was.

I ran back to the school yard for snack. The other girls were even more upset than when I left them. But I was very happy. After snack I invited the girl who was the most upset to come back and make dolls with me. I taught her how to make the dolls and soon she was happy again too.

I love to play by myself outside where we live in the country. I like to go exploring with Bokie, our dog, and build secret houses. These houses are under trees, up in trees, in the tall grasses or under bushes. I like to read, draw and do crafts in secret houses. Sometimes I don't do anything but listen to nature. I don't feel alone because the birds and Bokie keep me company. I know the fairies are there too. Also I have myself to play with. Sometimes I tell myself stories with different nature treasures. Sometimes I imagine stories while looking at the trees or clouds. I also like to tell stories while I am drawing.

It's also fun on different days to have my friends come over and play with me. My best friends also like to explore and build secret houses.

Whether I am alone, or with friends or my family, I like to be my own best friend. When I'm having a spelling test and do well I tell myself I did a great job. When I get up in the morning I say, "Good morning Rami," and I feel happy to be me. The day before my eleventh birthday I made myself a note and pinned it on the wall. The note said, "Good morning Rami and happy birthday. I love you so very much. Lots of love and joy. — Love Rami."

When I saw the note I felt so happy and jumped out of bed. That is how I started my wonderful birthday.

Loving myself has brought a lot of joy into my life. Sometimes it makes me want to just skip around the house laughing and singing.

Good morning Rami
and Happy Birthday.
I love you so very
much. Lots of love and
joy. Love Rami

LOVE MY FAMILY! I have quite a big family with all the animals. I have a loving mother and father, a little sister Mira who is six and a sister in the heaven world. Bokie, our brown dog is a lot of fun to play with. Pumpkin is my special cat. Turn-Up is a good mother cat and shy Milly is Mira's cat. We are a happy family of nine except when the kittens are born and then it's more like a farm. It's great to have a family to share life with. I like it when our grandmas and grandpas come to visit too.

At first our family was small. There was just my parents and me. I was the only child for five and a half years. Before Mira was born I was worried. I liked having my parents all to myself. I never had to share them. Now I would have to.

When she was born it was a lot of fun at first. I got to hold her, rock her and sing to her. I enjoyed pushing her in the buggy. My favorite was puppet shows. She followed the movements with her eyes.

But then it started to not be so much fun. She cried a lot and Mama had to spend a lot of time with her. The times Mira did sleep Mama was busy doing all of her work. I had to play by myself and I missed being with Mama.

One Saturday while Daddy was working late at the hospital, Mira cried very hard. That day she was only happy in the bathroom on the changing table kicking without her diapers. For some funny reason the bathroom was her favorite room and she was usually happy there as long as Mama was there with her. Poor Mama couldn't even leave to make our lunch. I decided I would surprise her and make lunch myself. I made a great fruit salad. I still remember how happy Mama was when I walked into the bathroom with a fruit salad and two bowls. We ate our lunch in the bathroom while Mira kicked and looked at her mobile.

It made me feel so good to help I decided to help more. Mira slept for a long time that day and Mama and I played with clay in the back yard. I felt very happy. Each day I did something to help and then Mama had time to play with me alone while Mira slept.

Soon we were having a lot of fun again. I helped Mama by playing with Mira. I taught

her to sit up by herself and then to crawl. Then I started teaching her how to talk and then how to walk. It was also my job to feed Mira her cereal. I laughed at how messy she was. Because I helped every day Mama had a special time with me while Mira napped. Soon I got to see that life was more fun since Mira came. Mira became my little friend and I

taught her all of my favorite games. Sometimes she even called me Mama. That made me feel very important. When she started talking a lot I was the only one who knew what she was trying to say. When she didn't want her supper, I'd pretend I wanted it and then she'd eat it all up.

Now that she is six years old we play a lot together. When we go places with our parents and there are only adults, I'm so glad Mira is around so we can play. Sometimes after dinner Mama and Daddy start talking about business and it is very boring. Mira and I go off then and start to giggle and pretend we are animals. We try and get Daddy to join us because he is a very good tiger.

Sometimes Mira and I fight and then it's not much fun to have a sister. Then I wonder if it would have been better if she would have never come. But soon the fight is over and we giggle again. It can be real hard with Mira, but mostly it's fun. I'm glad I have a sister.

* * * * * * *

I'M MIRA and I'm six years old. I don't know how to write yet, so I'm telling my story to Mama.

I love my family very much. I like to play with Rami. Our favorite game is rough-house with Daddy. Sometimes we get him to tickle us. He makes silly giggling noises. I have a special time in the morning with Mama before anyone else is up.

Sometimes when I want to play I go down to Rami's room and ask her what she would like to do. Rami has lots of good ideas. We usually play in my room and sometimes she lets me play in her room. We also have great games outside. When Grandma and Grandpa come we like to play games like Uno and Chinese checkers.

Rami takes care of me whenever Mama and Daddy are gone for a little while in the evening. She reads me stories, sings songs and puts me to sleep. Then it seems almost like she is my mother. I feel real safe with Rami.

But sometimes she tries too much to tell me what to do. I don't like it when she acts like a boss. Then I wish I were the oldest child in the family so she would know that it isn't a good feeling to be told what to do. I like it best when she is just my friend.

MIRA

Once Rami went skiing with a friend and I was alone. I missed her every day and couldn't wait until she came back. She was only gone for five days, but it seemed much longer. Then I was so happy to see her again. She brought me back a little present. I like it when Rami is home.

FOR MY HOMESCHOOL I read a book about a very great American Indian, Chief Seattle. He was a wonderful teacher to his people and loved all life. He is like a teacher to me too. When he signed the treaty with the white people, they told him he could have one thing in return for helping them. This is what he said:

"I will make one condition. The white man must treat the animals of this land as his brothers." He wanted us to love and be friends with all of the animals.

I love animals! They teach me so much and make my life happier. I think animals are fun.

Pumpkin is my big orange cat. He has white paws, a white tummy and a white tip at the end of his tail. His fur is long and soft. In the morning he meows (it sounds more like "maaa" as in "math") to get into the house. He runs at top speed to his kibble bowl. Sometimes he goes so fast he slips on the kitchen floor. Then he stops at his kibble bowl and won't eat until I give him a pat on his head. After he eats he tries to sneak up to my mom and dad's bed. My mom doesn't like him to be there and has told him many times, but each day he sneaks up anyway. He is shy of people and runs to me whenever anyone comes into our house.

Pumpkin is teaching me how to be a mother. I feel like he is my little son and I am very devoted to him. Pumpkin is also teaching me how to be patient, just like a mother has to be. Once we took him on our camping trip. Each night at 3 a.m. exactly, he scratched on the camper door wanting to get in. Everyone in the family was mad at him except for me. My dad yelled at him for ruining the screen door. My mother once threw water at him. Each night I got up and let him in. He walked around my bed and

around my head for a half hour then wanted to get out again. I had to get up again and let him out. Even though he did this each night for three weeks, I still loved him as my own son and thought he was cute. At the end of our camping trip we took a family vote and all voted to leave Pumpkin at home next time we went camping.

Whenever I feel sad I go and hug Pumpkin. We look at each other and he comforts me with his eyes. Pumpkin always makes me feel better.

Turn-Up is Pumpkin's sister. She is a calico cat. She is very different from Pumpkin. She doesn't like to be in the house, or be petted or picked up. We changed her name from Turnip to Turn-Up because she only turns up in the morning and evening for food, then wants to go right out again.

The best thing about Turn-Up is that she is a good mother. She has beautiful kittens and gives them a lot of love. Everyone always wants her kittens. We kept Milly, one of her orange kittens.

Milly is Mira's orange cat. She nursed on Turn-Up until she was bigger than her mother. Then Turn-Up would "hiss" her away. Milly still wanted to nurse so she pretended to nurse on Pumpkin. At first Pumpkin was surprised and didn't want her to. Then he let her. She would pretend to nurse, purring and moving her paws. He pretended to enjoy it, but really he wasn't so sure he liked it. Milly loves to be with Pumpkin. Pumpkin would rather be left alone to sleep.

Bokie is our family dog. He is a three-year-old golden retriever. He is a lot of fun and always wants to be with us. Everyone loves Bokie very much.

When he was about 10 months old we didn't like him very much. He was very clumsy and always got into trouble. When we would go for walks in the woods and on the beach he would run so fast and wild that he would crash into us. Once he knocked me into a big sticker bush. Once he ran so hard into Mira that she cried for an hour and wouldn't walk. The worst was when he ran in front of my mother while she was out jogging at night. He hit her so hard that she fell and broke her left elbow. He also dug up a lot of our flower gardens and then started on the lawn. He was trying to catch gophers. He would also sneak into the closet and eat up all of his dog treats.

My mom wondered if he was the right dog for us. Mira was afraid of him. I decided

I would love him into being a good boy. He was very wild and did everything wrong. At times it was hard to keep loving Bokie, but I knew he would be a good boy if I kept on loving him. Whenever Bokie was good (which wasn't very often), I told him what a good boy he was. I also talked to him and told him that we wanted him in our family, but he had to start behaving a little better. We all knew he wanted to behave, but he just didn't know how. Whenever he did something we didn't like, I always made him sit and then I looked him right in the eyes. Then I would tell him how he should behave. Whenever he dug in the garden I talked to him. Then I took him to an open field and showed him where he could dig.

Slowly he began to learn. He only dug in the fields and ran around us during the walks rather than into us. Then we started telling him he was the best dog in the world. He

liked that, and tried even harder to please us. Now he is so well-behaved we can't even remember the last time we had to yell at him. Whenever I go off by myself to play he always comes with me. He is a great friend to all of us. I hope I can always have a golden dog friend.

Our neighbors raise calves. They usually have at least thirty calves. They go to the auction and buy them. They are taken from their mothers when they are very young. The calves cry a lot when they are first brought here. They miss their mothers. They are so cute and Mira and I love them a lot. Sometimes Marie, our neighbor, lets us feed them a bottle. While they drink I pet them softly. Calves are very tender animals with feelings. They like to be loved and petted. Their eyes are so caring and their fur so soft. Their breath is very sweet too. I have a favorite calf, whose name is Butterscotch. He is the smallest calf and the others seem to push him around. So Mira and I give him lots of attention.

Our neighbors also have a mother cow named Clarabelle. When I was in second grade, Clarabelle had a little calf named Judy. Clarabelle had so much milk that there was lots left over. Marie gave us an extra gallon each day and I took it to school. The children were so happy that they all made little cards to hang around Clarabelle's neck. Clarabelle was very proud to have all the cards around her neck.

About twice a year we hear a loud gun shot, and we know that they have killed another cow. Then it is cut into meat. We all feel very sad and say a prayer for the cow. I feel then that one of my friends has been killed. Someday it might be Butterscotch. I don't eat meat because I don't want to be eating one of my friends.

I love the birds and enjoy hearing them sing and feed at our bird feeder. I love the squirrels that climb on the trees, the bees that make honey and the butterflies that make my garden so pretty. I love the deer that come to eat our apples and the sound of the coyotes barking at night. I love the beautiful owls that hoot in the night and the hawks that soar through the sky. Even the little mice that come to visit us in our house are really very cute.

All animals are beautiful and special. They help our world be a happier place. Animals are really great friends.

Angels blessing the worl

AT FIRST, when my parents told me we were going to have another baby, I was very excited. They told me the baby might come on my birthday, March 26th. A few days later I was unsure about having another baby in the family. I remembered that when Mira was a baby she cried a lot and I had to play by myself. But then I got excited again when my mother took out all the little baby clothes that Mira and I used to wear. I knew that I would be a mother to the baby.

When my mother's tummy started growing I used to hug the baby and talk to it. I knew this baby would be special and I felt a lot of love for her. Even though everyone thought we'd have a boy, I felt the baby was a girl. After Christmas I was going to make her a beautiful doll. I felt joy and happiness inside whenever I thought about a new little sister.

On Christmas Eve it felt like the Christ child was being born in our family because my mother was pregnant. It was a happy Christmas. A few days after Christmas I got sick and had to stay home from a party. My father and Mira went with Grandma and Grandpa. My mother and I had a cozy time by the Christmas tree. It seemed like we could hear the angels singing. We talked a lot about the baby. My mom told me she was sure we were having a girl and her name was Anjel. Suddenly I no longer felt sick and I jumped up and danced around the tree. A baby sister was my dream come true. I felt so happy I could have burst with joy. This was the last totally happy time I had for awhile.

The next day our midwife came. She knew a lot about babies. While Mira, Daddy and I sat around Mama, she examined the baby. Then her face looked worried and she said Mama needed a special test. Right away my parents, Mira and I went to the hospital. Daddy said that the test helps to see how the baby is growing and moving. I was worried. It seemed like something was wrong. While Daddy was filling out some papers for the test, Mama went to the waiting room. Mira and I sat by Daddy. Even though the voice in my heart told me everything would be all right, I still felt sad. Daddy looked worried and sad too. Mira didn't seem to understand, but she was sucking her thumb which she hardly ever does.

Finally we went to the exam room. Mama was already there lying on a bed. The doctor put some cream on Mama's belly and then the instrument to see inside. They looked very worried and told us the baby had died. I couldn't stand the sadness anymore and burst out crying. My mom was crying too. Mira tried to comfort Mama by saying, "I'd rather have a brother than no baby at all." Mira was so cute that we stopped crying for a minute and held each other. We were thankful to have each other. After Daddy talked with the doctor we all sat together and loved each other.

Grandpa and Grandma came and got Mira and me and took us home. Mama and Daddy went to another doctor.

The next day Daddy took Mama to the hospital to have the baby's body removed. Grandma sat with Mira and me and told us we would pray for Mama. She taught us the 23rd Psalm about God being a Good Shepherd watching over us. The prayers made me feel good and close to Grandma.

23rd Psalm

The Lord is my shepherd, I shall not want.
He makes me lie down in green pastures.
He leads me beside still waters.
He restores my soul.
He leads me in paths of righteousness
　　　for His name's sake.

And even though I walk through the valley
　　　of the shadow of death, I fear no evil;
For You are with me;
Your rod and your staff comfort me.

You prepare a table before me
　　　in the presence of my enemies.
You anoint my head with oil.
My cup overflows.

Surely goodness and mercy shall follow me
　　　all the days of my life, and I shall dwell
　　　in the house of the Lord forever.

Then I went and climbed a tree to wait for Mama. Different trees give you different gifts when you climb and sit in them. Our big fir tree makes me feel close to the heavens. Oak trees help me to pray better. Redwood trees are peaceful trees. We can also feel the tree by hugging it, but that is not as good as climbing it. That day I chose a long- needled pine tree because it gives me strength and courage. As I sat in the pine tree I felt strong and full of courage to face the sadness. Soon I heard a car and I saw Mama. I quickly climbed down and ran to meet her and Daddy.

I spent the rest of the day lying in bed with Mama. I was glad she was home again. I wasn't as sad as when we had first found out that Anjel had died, but I still wasn't happy.

That night some friends came with supper for us. I played wild games with the two boys my age. It felt good to run and jump, scream and be wild. I was having so much fun I forgot about being sad. Whenever I'm sad, it always helps to run around outside with a friend.

I went to bed early that night and woke in the middle of the night. Something was different and I couldn't go back to sleep. I wanted to wake up my parents but I thought I shouldn't since I didn't have a good reason. Then I felt a little pain in my ear. I ran through the dark of our house and opened their door. I was so surprised to see them sitting up in bed. Then I said, "I have an earache."

Mama started laughing softly and said, "You don't have an earache. You are feeling all the prayers being said around the world for peace." I smiled and happily got into bed with them.

This night, December 31, 1986, was the first world peace meditation. Millions of people all over the world were praying for peace at the exact same hour. Our time in California was 4 a.m. We had a very close time together. As we prayed for peace and started thinking about others, Anjel came very close to us. It felt almost like we could reach out and touch her. I could feel her love and I knew she would always be with me. I felt how special it was to have a sister in the heaven world. As I was praying and thanking God for Anjel, it felt like I heard her tell me that she would help me in many ways. An important way is helping me to write this book.

The next day my father brought home the dead little body from the hospital. I was surprised it would look like that. I always felt Anjel to be so big and beautiful and this little body was so small and strange looking. I realized that the body wasn't so important. It was the spirit that was important. Then I knew that I was more than my body too. I was a great spirit that came down from the heaven world to live in this body.

For the next several days it felt like Anjel was sleeping right in bed with me. She was so close to me in the daytime, too, and followed me everywhere I went. She seemed to be saying to me that she would never leave me and would always be close.

Later on I got real sad. I wanted to hold my sister. This lasted a few weeks. Sometimes I went down to my room and cried. Other times I just wanted to be alone outside. It always helped me to climb or hug a tree.

Then our family went to Yosemite National Park for a short winter camping trip. When we first got to the park there was a lot of snow in the campground. We hitched up our dog Bokie to our toboggan and he took us for wild rides along the icy roads. It was so much fun and Bokie was so silly that Mira and I laughed very hard. I didn't feel sad anymore.

On the the last day of the trip we went to Bridalveil Falls. I hiked up the steep rocks to be very close to the falls. Daddy, Mira and Mama stayed back. I found a little protected place away from all the mist and stood look-ing at the falls. The more I looked, the more I began to see the form of an angel. Finally I saw a shining being of light in the falls and I knew it must be Anjel. We stood just looking

at each other. Then she told me not to be sad anymore because she would always be there with me. She had so much peace in her words that I felt peaceful too. Before, I felt sad be-cause I wanted to hold my sister. Now I knew she would be holding me in her love.

Then my father called me to come down and I couldn't see her anymore. But I knew she was with me.

E WERE CAMPED at our favorite camping place last Father's Day. It was a happy day and Mira and I made cards for Daddy. Mine had a drawing of him with Mira and me. I also wrote a poem which was on the inside. Our very good friends, Bobbi and John, came to visit us for two days. During breakfast I gave Daddy my card. He was so happy and loved the card so much. Mama asked me to read the poem to everyone. Everyone said they really wanted to hear it.

Suddenly I felt shy. It wasn't a good feeling. I was afraid to talk and looked at the table. Everyone wanted to hear my poem, which made me feel even worse. This has happened to me at other times in my life. Someone would want me to talk and I would feel too scared and not know what to do. I felt sad and walked away. I walked into the woods and the trees comforted me.

After a long time I came back and Bobbi found me. She gave me a big hug and made me feel better. Bobbi is a very happy person and always has something kind to say to everyone. She is a doctor's assistant and knows a lot about bones and muscles. She is also my yoga teacher. Bobbi told me she'd help me learn to enjoy talking to other people. I've always enjoyed talking to my parents and Mira and other children. It was just hard with adults. She told me a great story.

Later, we all went sailing. On the sailing trip my mother and I had a good idea for a point system. I would earn a point towards something I really wanted each time I talked to someone outside of our family. I really wanted this special thing, and I also wanted to get over my shyness, so I was really willing to try the point system.

When we got back the sun was setting. I felt happy inside and also excited to build a big campfire. Bobbi and I went into the woods to gather firewood. Most of the wood was very dry, so we could break it very easily by jumping on it. We both found a large branch. I decided to jump on it to break it in half. The branch must have just fallen for it was very springy. I didn't know that. When I jumped on it, it was like a trampoline and bounced me right back off. I fell on my right arm. I felt so much pain in my arm that I screamed. Bobbi came running to me. She asked me to move off of my arm.

When I moved, it hurt even more. She helped me walk down to where Daddy had the campfire going. I was in a lot of pain and crying. Everyone came running. Bobbi rubbed oil on my arm and tried to find out by touching in different places if it was broken. She thought it was and made a special cast for me out of cardboard and tape. The nearest hospital was two hours away over mountain roads and since it was late we decided to go the next day. I had an awful night because my arm hurt so much. Even my cat Pumpkin couldn't cheer me up that time.

Early the next morning I left with my Dad to go to the hospital. They took X-rays and found I had a break in my right arm close to my wrist. I needed a cast for six weeks. While the doctor was casting my arm he asked me how I broke it. I knew I had to tell the story by myself and so I did. After I finished telling him I felt very proud. When the nurse came in she wanted to know my story too. Again I told the same long story. Afterwards I looked at Daddy and he winked at me. Daddy was proud of me too. I knew I had just earned two points.

We came back late in the evening to where Mama and Mira were waiting by the campfire. I showed them the X-ray of my broken bone.

The next day I figured out a way to go swimming. I wrapped my arm in plastic bags and floated it on an air mattress. I could still have fun in the water, but not as much.

A few days later, we left to go back east to visit Grandma and Grandpa. The moment we got to the airport, people started asking me how I broke my arm. The check-in lady wanted to know, the stewardess sat down next to me and wanted to hear the story, and even the pilot called me into the cockpit and asked me to tell him how I broke my arm. Then he told me how he had broken his arm once. I earned so many points for talking just on the first day of traveling.

Wherever we went the next week, people wanted to hear my story. In just seven days I had collected sixty points for talking. I was talking so much about my arm that I forgot all about being shy. Each time I talked I got

braver about talking. I found out it was really fun to talk.

The night before my cast was to be taken off, I rubbed my arm and cast lovingly. I felt that the broken arm had really helped me a lot. I realized that there had been a great hidden blessing for me in breaking my arm. There must be a hidden blessing in everything that seems bad.

ALL SUMMER I was very excited to go on our first river rafting trip. Finally the big day came. We drove to the Klamath River in Northern California where we met the other people on the trip. We had a big campfire that night and talked about our five-day trip starting the next morning. We had six special river guides: David, Jane, Steve, Paula, Matt and Lloyd. They told us how to pack our "black bags", waterproof bags for holding our clothes and things. We were told to bring as little as possible. I was sad to leave my pillow behind.

The next day Matt gave a safety talk. He told us most accidents happen on land, not in the water or in the rafts. The talk was very funny. Steve talked about the kayaks, which are small boats for one or two people. I wanted to try a kayak but I felt nervous. What if I tipped over?

When the group started out I was in the big raft with Steve, my mom, dad, Mira and Bokie our dog. We all had life-jackets on except Bokie. Bokie looked scared on the first rapid, but then he settled down and enjoyed the trip. The guides had made a special platform for him covered with netting on top of the supplies. He could lie there with his claws holding on to the netting and look at the five other boats and six kayaks.

That afternoon, Heidi, a junior guide, asked me to ride in a kayak with her. At first I didn't want to because I felt scared. But then I decided it would be fun. It was fun! Next, I wanted to try riding the kayak by myself. I was worried though. What if I tipped over going down one of the big rapids? Would I come back up? Would I bump a big rock? Would it hurt? I was scared.

Then I decided I needed to be brave. I said to myself over and over again, "I am brave. I am brave." I decided to try a kayak the next day.

That night as I lay on the ground in my sleeping bag, I thought about kayaking by myself. I still felt worried about tipping over but I tried to imagine myself being brave.

The next day was a layover day. A layover day means that we stayed in one place. My mom and dad gave the workshop all morning. In the afternoon I practiced kayaking in the still water. It was so much fun.

The next day I decided to go down the river by myself. The river guides told me that the first rapid was gentle. It was easy to go over and I was very proud of myself. I kayaked that whole day. Whenever I would

worry about a big rapid that was coming up, I would say to myself, "I am brave."

Each day I went by myself in the kayak. I found I was not only getting brave but also sometimes bold. There were places where the river was calm and people had water-splashing fights. Boldly I splashed people. I even splashed David, our head river guide. He was amazed that I could be so daring. He smiled and splashed me back.

On the last day of the trip we came to a very scary rapid. At first I thought it would be like any of the other rapids, until I saw the big waves. Then it was too late. I couldn't stop. I felt nervous and scared. What if the kayak tipped? I started to say, "I am brave," but before I knew it I was tipped into the water. I grabbed my paddle and started swimming to shore. Then I found out it was really fun. I took my time and enjoyed the waves, remembering to keep my feet up like the guides told me.

When I joined the group I had a big smile on my face. I got right out of the river and ran back upstream to jump in the rapid again. Tipping over was the most fun part of the trip for me. What I worried would be the worst part, turned out to be the best.

Plants And Nature Spirits

PART OF MY HOMESCHOOL is vegetable and flower gardening. A nice man named Steve is my gardening teacher. He comes every week to teach me. Everything we use is natural.

We never kill gophers. We ask them to leave. Sometimes it works. Sometimes it doesn't. We tried putting up a sign asking them to eat someplace else. It worked for awhile, but then they came back and ate a cabbage. Then there were only two cabbages left. One was a good one, one wasn't. I tried to trick the gophers, so I said in a loud voice, "I sure hope the gophers don't eat this cabbage," as I pointed to the bad one. The next day the bad one was gone and the good one was left. Gophers are the only part of gardening that is not much fun.

I have grown lots of different vegetables and beautiful flowers. My favorite are the many-colored sweet peas. I like to pick them for my mother to put on the kitchen table.

I like to come out and sit in my garden. If I sit long enough and stay very still I see a little flash of fairy wings or a little red hat peeping out from the vegetables. Gnomes wear red hats. They help flowers and vegetables to grow.

Once I picked a flower and looked down and saw a tiny fairy. She told me that she loved me and wanted to be my friend.

Once, when I was by a tree, I saw a tiny little man and he was chopping on a rock, trying to open it. I asked him why he was doing that and he answered, "Because I am a gnome and am looking for precious stones." He had a little house. He became my close little friend.

Once on my birthday, the little gnome gave me a special stone. I keep it in a special place.

The gnomes and fairies have brought me a lot of joy. That is why I love flowers so much.

— RAMI, FROM MODELS OF LOVE:
THE PARENT-CHILD JOURNEY

The fairies give the flowers their beautiful colors. Sometimes if you are very lucky you can see a plant with two different colored flowers. You can know then that the fairies have kissed that plant. When I was little I could see the fairies very clearly. They always made me very happy. Fairies love little children, and enjoy watching them play and dance. Little children have just come from the heaven world and are surrounded by angels.

Fairies like to be near the angels.

Now that I am bigger I can't see the fairies as clearly. But I can still see their little spark of light as they dance around. I can also

sense their presence in my heart as they make me feel warm and beautiful. Fairies love flowers the best. Whenever someone stops to smell a flower they will be blessed by a fairy.

If you would like to make friends with a fairy or a gnome, here is a good way to do it:

1. Sit in a garden with beautiful flowers or vegetables, or sit in the woods, perhaps near a stream or waterfall. Fairies like flowers and moving water.

2. Be very quiet and still. Close your eyes for a few minutes. Listen to the birds singing and all the nature sounds.

3. Then still with your eyes closed whisper to the fairies and tell them that you love them and would very much like to see them. Feel thankful for all of the beauty that the fairies help to create.

4. When you are feeling very grateful for the flowers open your eyes and you just might see a fairy or see a flash of their wings.

Even if you don't see one, you can still feel their happy presence which will make you want to smile. Don't be discouraged if you don't see one right away. It takes practice. Just spend a little time each day and sit quietly in the same place or a new place. After awhile you may be blessed to see one. Then you will always know that you have special fairy friends.

THE ANGELS are very close to us. We can't always see them, but they are always there to help us.

When I was almost seven years old my Grandma and Grandpa (my mother's parents) came from Buffalo to visit at Christmas. They took care of a big house while the people went away. Grandma and Grandpa wanted me to come and spend the night. At first I didn't want to, but mama and daddy wanted me to. I worried about spending the night away from home. I had never been away from my parents overnight before. I was afraid I wouldn't be able to go to sleep.

Finally, the day came when I was going to spend the night with Grandma and Grandpa. Everyone was very excited about this except me. I felt nervous and didn't want to go. Mama helped me pack my little suitcase. I brought my favorite teddy bear. Then Mama, Daddy, Mira and I drove to where Grandma and Grandpa were staying.

Everyone talked and had a good time at dinner. I almost forgot that I was going to spend the night, but not quite. I was still nervous. Then Mama, Daddy and Mira left and I was alone with Grandma and Grandpa. Grandpa and I played cards and I laughed a lot . I was having such a good time I even forgot I was going to spend the night. Then Grandma announced it was time for bed. Suddenly I got very scared. Grandma said she would sleep with me. I was glad but still felt scared.

Lying in bed, Grandma soon fell sound asleep and was snoring loudly. I felt very lonely for my own bed and my parents. I said a little prayer that I could go to sleep and that I could feel happy. After my prayer I thought I heard someone calling my name. I looked and it sure wasn't Grandma because she was sound asleep. Then I heard a soft, tender voice that said "I am your guardian angel, Rami. I am always with you. Go to sleep and I will make your dreams happy." I went right to sleep and my dreams were happy.

In the morning I woke up and Grandma was already out of bed. I had a very happy day making cookies to bring to Mama. Whenever I'm scared now, I remember that my angel will always be with me.

Sometimes my mother and I don't get along very well. After we have yelled at each other I go off to a secret place to be alone. One day Mama yelled at me because she thought I wasn't helping very much. I thought she

didn't notice how much I had done. I went off to my secret place in nature. I started to cry. After a while I stopped crying and realized I could ask my guardian angel for help. I closed my eyes and was quiet for a few minutes. Then I asked silently for help to get along better with my mother. I opened my eyes and saw a light. The light looked very faintly like an angel. I knew my guardian

angel was there. I could hear her sweet voice in my heart telling me to go back and hug my mother. Then the light was gone. I could no longer see her light, but I knew she was still with me, smiling and helping me.

I walked up the hill and into the house. I saw my mother and we both hugged each other. Then together we washed the dishes and both of us felt happy.

Everyone has a special guardian angel that is there to help them. The angels also help the animals. When our dog Kriya died I could feel the angels. They were taking her spirit to the heaven world. When Turn-Up was having her kittens I could feel the angels bringing each spirit into the little kitten body.

Our guardian angel is always by our side. Whenever we need help all we have to do is pray to our angel and wait to feel the help. Our angel loves us very much and wants to see us happy. It's great to know that we have such a special friend. Don't forget to thank your angel for all the wonderful help. Angels love to feel our love too!

Prayer to my Guardian Angel

Dear Guardian Angel,
Thank you for staying close and protecting me
Thank you for helping me make the right decisions
Thank you for helping me to be loving
Thank you for showing me the ways to be happy
and to make other people happy
Thank you for loving me so much.

Amen

The earth is our Mother,
She gives us good food.
The sun is our Father,
He gives us warm light.
The stars are all our brothers and sisters,
And the moon guides us along.

So don't you know how lucky you are,
To have so many friends.

The Mother That Is Always There

DID YOU KNOW that you have a beautiful mother that is always loving and caring for you? She is there even when you feel like you are alone. You can't always see her, but you can feel her love in your heart. She is our Heavenly Mother, and is a mother to all of us. Knowing how much She loves you can make you feel good all over.

When I was a little girl my mother started telling me about all the heavenly beings that looked after me. She especially talked about my Heavenly Mother. It didn't really make sense to me. It was hard to believe that I had a Heavenly Mother that loved me when I could see my own mother.

I thought my own mother could do everything and would always be there. My mother told me that sometimes she couldn't always be there but that my Heavenly Mother could. She told me that whenever I needed help I could pray to Her. It was hard for me to understand but I trusted that my mother was telling the truth.

When I was six I found out for myself that my Heavenly Mother *is* always there. We went on a camping trip to our favorite lake. We were totally alone. My sister Mira was just a new baby and needed lots of care and attention. My mother and father were very busy with Mira, so I often played alone with our dog Kriya. One day while Mira was crying and my parents were changing her diaper, I decided to get some peace and quiet. I called Kriya to come for a walk. We went through the meadow and crossed a little stream. I played at the stream for awhile and then continued up the meadow. I picked wild flowers as I went. Soon I came to a woods and kept walking. Kriya followed and I felt very happy. I even skipped a little.

After awhile, I felt I should go back to our camp spot. I looked around and discovered I was lost. I had no idea which way to go. Everything looked the same. I asked Kriya how we should go back. She lay down and just looked up at me. She wanted more of an adventure. I knew she wouldn't help me get back home.

I sat down on a rock and started to cry. Kriya came very close to comfort me. After a while I realized crying wouldn't help so I started screaming as loud as I could. The screaming didn't help either because my parents couldn't hear me.

Then I remembered what my parents had said about my Heavenly Mother. I thought I would try asking for Her help. I closed my eyes and tried to imagine what a Heavenly Mother would look like. Then I asked if She would please help me to get back to my parents. I sat with my eyes closed for a short time trying to hear Her talk to me. I couldn't hear anything except the singing of birds and Kriya's breathing. But when I opened my eyes I could hardly believe what I saw. There was a light golden mist hardly touching the ground. It led in one direction and I knew I must follow it. It disappeared behind me as I walked. I felt so light and happy as I walked along. I followed the

golden mist all the way back to our camp. When I looked back there was nothing but the meadow.

I ran to my mother and hugged her tight. Mira had cried a long time and had just fallen asleep. My parents had just started looking for me. We were all very happy. Now I know that I *do* have a wonderful Heavenly Mother. We all have the same great Mother and she is always with us.

At other hard times in my life she has come and comforted me. She comes to me in happy times too. She comes whenever I need her. She is always loving me and loving you too!

I thought of ten ways to get closer to our Heavenly Mother:

1. Smell a flower and know that the fragrance is Her perfume and that She is very close.

2. Go out in nature and listen to the nature sounds. Sit very still and listen to the birds, the wind through the trees, the sounds of water and forest creatures. Know that this is Her favorite music and She is also listening with you.

3. Sit alone and be very quiet. Feel how much you need the Heavenly Mother's love and ask Her to help you feel Her love in your heart. She will make you feel warm and happy.

4. Say a prayer to Her at night before you go to sleep and ask that you can have a special dream with Her. She loves to come in dreams and say special things.

5. Think of Her in the morning and know that She will be your special friend all day long.

6. Appreciate and love other people and know She is smiling at you as you do.

7. Say nice things to yourself and keep telling yourself what a good job you are doing. She wants us to love ourselves as much as She loves us.

8. Thank Her for all of the Blessings in your life.

9. Look into other people's faces and see the Heavenly Mother smiling back at you.

10. Imagine the most perfect father you could ever have. This is your Heavenly Father. When you thank Him for being there this brings your Heavenly Mother very close to you, and makes Her very happy.

The earth is our Mother,
She gives us good food.
The sun is our Father,
He gives us warm light.
The stars are all our brothers and sisters,
And the moon guides us along.

So don't you know how lucky you are,
To have so many friends.

The earth is loving you,
The sun is loving you,
The stars are loving you,
And the moon is loving you.

So don't you know how much you are
Loved.

Other Books by Rami's Family

THE SHARED HEART: Relationship Initiations and Celebrations by Barry and Joyce Vissell

(Rami illustrated this book when she was seven; includes the powerful story of her birth.)

A relationship bestseller! This book has touched the hearts of many thousands. "A map of the relationship journey." —RAM DASS *"...full to overflowing with immeasurable guidelines on using our relationships as tools for our further awakening."* —SCIENCE OF THOUGHT REVIEW, England. *"Offers the transpersonal perspective to relationship, integrating ancient wisdom and modern psychological theory ... the Vissells show how to follow a path of consciousness while in committed relationship"* —THE COMMON BOUNDARY

ISBN 0-9612720-0-7 $9.95

MODELS OF LOVE: The Parent-Child Journey by Joyce and Barry Vissell

(Rami's first writing adventure; includes her touching chapter about her dog's death and other stories, poems and many illustrations.)

A powerful, heart-warming testament to the way parents and children may bring love and peace to the world. Foreword by Eileen Caddy of Findhorn and contributions by 17 others including Leo Buscaglia, Joan Hodgson, Gerald Jampolsky, Qahira Qalbi and Jack Kornfield. An exceptional manual for the journey of parenting.

"...full of miraculous incidents and sacred moment of loving connection that will bring tears to your eyes...the valuable lessons and insights of MODELS OF LOVE can be appreciated by both parents and non-parents alike." —THE WHOLE LIFE MONTHLY.

ISBN 0-9612720-1-5 $10.95

RISK TO BE HEALED: The Heart of Personal and Relationship Growth by Barry and Joyce Vissell

Here is what Hugh Prather, referred to as "an American Kahlil Gibran" by the New York Times, says about *Risk To Be Healed:* *"In this book, Joyce & Barry offer the priceless gift of their own experience with relationship, commitment, vulnerability, sorrow and loss, along with a profound guide to healing that comes from the core of their being and blesses us with gentle wisdom."*

"Nothing bashful about these folks. They celebrate their tears, their hearts, and many discoveries." —The Book Reader

ISBN 0-9612720-2-3 $9.95

The above books or *Rami's Book* may be ordered directly from:

RAMIRA PUBLISHING
P.O. Box 1707, Aptos, CA 95001
(408) 684-2299 or TOLL FREE 1-800-766-0629

• QUANTITY DISCOUNT: 20% for 5 or more items

• Shipping: $2 first item, $1 each additional item

• California residents please add sales tax

For information about Joyce and Barry's cassette tapes on relationship and family, other heart-offerings from Ramira Publishing, or the Vissell's schedule of workshops and retreats for individuals, couples or families, write to Ramira Publishing.